Wonderful Welsh Sporting Heroes

To all the volunteers across Wales
who give their time to help children
discover the joy of sport.

First impression: 2025

© James Stafford & Y Lolfa Cyf., 2025

This book is subject to copyright and may not be reproduced by any means except for review purposes without the prior written consent of the publishers.

The publishers wish to acknowledge the support of the Books Council of Wales.

Cover design: Richard Huw Pritchard
All illustrations © Telor Gwyn
Design: Richard Huw Pritchard

ISBN: 978-1-80099-401-0

Published and printed in Wales
on paper from well-maintained forests by
Y Lolfa Cyf., Talybont, Ceredigion SY24 5HE
e-mail ylolfa@ylolfa.com
website www.ylolfa.com
tel 01970 832 304

Wonderful Welsh Sporting Heroes

James Stafford

Illustrated by
Telor Gwyn

Contents

Introduction

Wales is a small nation. Its three million people make up just 0.04% of the planet's entire population.

Despite this, we have an awful lot to be proud of in the world of sport. From the steepest of streets, the muddiest of fields, the smelliest of gyms and the coldest of waters, Wales has forged athletes to rival the best any nation can offer.

Yet too many Welsh sporting heroes are quickly forgotten about or aren't truly admired whilst they're competing. Hopefully this book can play a small part in changing that.

So, dive in and learn about the Welsh woman who won glory by swimming with whales, the tiny boxer who packed the punch of a giant, and the footballer who's been worshipped in Italy for generations. From stars you've cheered on in stadiums and on the telly, to long-gone heroes you've probably never even heard of, this book has them all.

Perhaps, after reading it, you may even be inspired to become a wonderful Welsh sporting hero yourself!

GARETH BALE

Wales's global superstar

Born: Cardiff, 16 July 1989

Sport: football

Position: winger, left back

Main clubs: Southampton, Tottenham Hotspur, Real Madrid, Los Angeles FC

Club goals: 141

Wales caps: 111

Wales goals: 41

Major honours include:

- La Liga winner x 3
- Champions League winner x 5
- Most-capped male Wales international
- Wales's all-time top male goalscorer
- FIFA Club World Cup Golden Ball
- Welsh Footballer of the Year x 6
- BBC Cymru Wales Sports Personality of the Year

1

With football such a huge part of global culture, **Gareth Bale** is possibly the most famous Welsh person of all time.

2

Gareth was born in Cardiff, and he was so far ahead of his classmates in football at school that his teacher made him only use his weaker right foot and always shoot or pass with his first touch of the ball! By age 9, he was being chased by professional clubs, eventually signing with Southampton.

He made his professional debut for Southampton aged 16, scoring his first goal a few months later. In his early career, he played as a defender (left back) and quickly established himself as a free-kick specialist. He scored plenty of exciting swerving goals with his deadly free-kick technique.

A true school of excellence

Steve Williams, Gareth's PE teacher at Whitchurch High School in Cardiff, amazingly also taught Wales and British & Irish Lions rugby captain Sam Warburton and Tour de France-winning cyclist Geraint Thomas (**see page 15**)!

European adventures

When Wales qualified for Euro 2016, nobody expected them to do much. Yet, thanks in huge part to Gareth, they stormed all the way to the semi-final. The Dragons' 3–1 win over star-studded Belgium in the quarter finals is one of the most celebrated nights in the history of Welsh sport.

3

After Gareth moved to Tottenham Hotspur, his manager decided to play him on the wing. In this position, Gareth became one of the world's leading players. His combination of speed (he was among the fastest players in the game), strength, stamina and ball control made him a nightmare for opposing teams and he regularly began to score spectacular goals.

4

In 2013, Gareth was signed by Spanish giants Real Madrid for a world-record fee of £85.3 million. He won 19 trophies with them, including five Champions League titles. Gareth had a habit of scoring his most impressive goals in big matches. His key goals in Real Madrid's Copa del Rey victory and the 2018 Champions League final (where he scored twice against Liverpool) will never be forgotten by the team's fans.

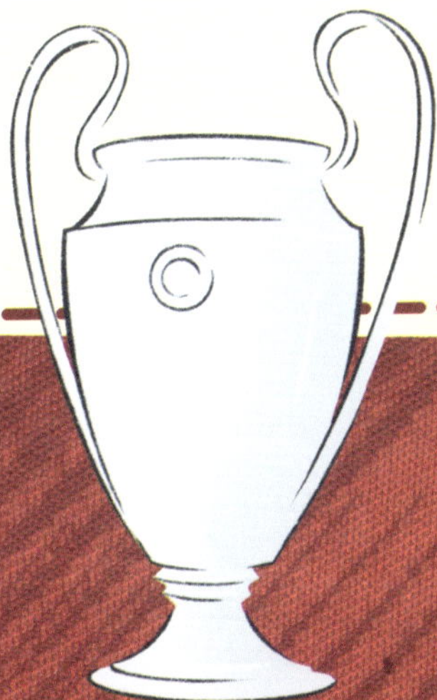

5

Gareth, an incredibly proud Welshman, won his first cap for Wales just before his 17th birthday. At the time he was the youngest player ever to represent Wales. He won 111 caps (a men's record!) and steered Wales to the semi-finals of Euro 2016 – Wales's first major tournament for decades. Gareth also helped Wales reach Euro 2020 and the 2022 World Cup – only Wales's second-ever World Cup, 64 years after the first.

6

Gareth was considered good luck for the Wales team, inspiring everyone to play their very best. His 41 goals for Wales are a men's national record – 13 ahead of the next highest scorer, Ian Rush!

Did you know?

- Wales's first international match was in 1876.
- Wales is the third oldest international team in the world.
- Only England and Scotland are older. Their first official match was against each other in 1872.

LAUREN PRICE

The girl who made her dreams come true

Born: Newport, 25 June 1994

Sports: boxing, kickboxing, football

Football: 2 Wales caps

Kickboxing:

- World Champion x 4
- European Champion x 6

Boxing (middleweight):

- Olympic gold
- European Games gold
- Commonwealth gold
- World Championships gold
- Undisputed World Female Welterweight Champion

2

When she was 8, Lauren's teacher asked her to write down her goals. Lauren wrote:

- Play football for Wales
- Be a kickboxing World Champion
- Compete in the Olympic Games

✓ Perhaps her teacher smiled when she saw it, but Lauren went on to achieve all three!

1

Lauren Price is really, really good at sport! Born in Newport, she was raised by her grandparents in Ystrad Mynach. Little did they know that encouraging her to use her amazing energy for sport would make her an Olympic and World Champion!

Learning from other sports

Lauren is a great example of how playing different sports helps people become better athletes. In football, she could kick the ball a lot further because of her kickboxing.

3

Encouraged by her grandad, she took up kickboxing as a child. At just 13, she won a silver World Championship medal, against opponents twice her age. She eventually won six European titles and four World Championships in the sport.

Bouncing like Tigger

Lauren's family called her 'Tigger' after the bouncing tiger from Winnie the Pooh, as she had endless energy. One of the reasons Lauren got to try so many sports was that her grandparents wanted to tire her out!

4

Lauren took part in other sports like netball, taekwondo and football. She played for Cardiff City, helping them to win the Welsh Premier Women's Football League, and won two senior caps for Wales (52 caps in total at all age group levels). She did this despite having to work long hours in various jobs as there wasn't much money in women's football at the time.

5

In 2014 she decided to focus on boxing and in the same year became the first Welsh woman to win a boxing medal: Commonwealth Games bronze. Lauren, fighting as a middleweight (up to 75 kg in weight), went on to add European and Commonwealth boxing gold medals to her impressive trophy cabinet.

In 2020 she was selected for Great Britain for the Tokyo Olympics, and grabbed gold. After the fight, she looked up to the sky and thought of her beloved grandad, who had sadly died the year before. Lauren was really happy that the phonebox outside her nan's house would be painted gold in celebration – because every time her nan opened the curtains, she'd see it!

Did you know?

- Women's boxing at the Olympics officially began in 2012.
- The first record of a female boxer is from 1722, when a London newspaper published a letter from Elizabeth Wilkinson challenging Hannah Hyfield to box her.
- In those days, boxers fought without gloves and after Elizabeth won the fight, she earned the nickname 'Lady Bareknuckles'.

6

Lauren shows what can be achieved with dedication and hard work. She was only the third Welsh woman to win solo Olympic gold, following in the footsteps of Jade Jones (**see page 52**) and Nicole Cooke (**see page 58**). Lauren turned professional in 2022 and in May 2024 she became World Champion.

GERAINT THOMAS

The Welsh cyclist who rode to the top of his sport

Born: Cardiff, 25 May 1986

Sport: cycling (road and track)

Main clubs: Team Sky/Ineos Grenadiers, Barloworld, Maindy Flyers Youth Cycling Club/CC Cardiff

Major honours include:

- Tour de France winner
- Olympic gold x 2
- World Championships gold x 3
- British National Road Race Championships gold
- National Time Trial Championships winner
- British Sports Personality of the Year

1

Wales is not known for its world-class cyclists. But the stupendous **Geraint Thomas** has proved himself one of the best cyclists in the world on both road and track.

2

After being taught to ride by his dad on a second-hand bike, Geraint fell in love with cycling. He joined Cardiff's Maindy Flyers Youth Cycling Club aged 10. Pretty soon he was winning races and showing glimpses of his talent and hard work. He loved being able to travel around the country on his bike and he built his fitness by spending hours riding the hills of south Wales in all kinds of cold and miserable weather.

Learning from defeat

Although Geraint finished 140th in his first Tour de France, the race was crucial to his development. Afterwards he said, "I was never going to get off. I was always going to try and get to the end... Getting through was a big boost for my morale."

3

In his teens, Geraint was invited by British Cycling to be part of its development academy. He won several major races and quickly repaid their faith.

4

Geraint's early successes came mainly in track cycling. He was part of the legendary British team that stormed to a gold medal in both the 2008 and 2012 Olympic team pursuit, where four riders race together over 4 km (2. 5 miles) against another team.

Crashes, bumps and breaks

Cycling is dangerous and Geraint has had lots of injuries!

- He had to have his spleen removed in 2005 after a crash.
- He broke his pelvis and fractured his nose in 2009.
- He broke his collarbone in 2017.
- He broke his pelvis again in 2020.

5

As amazing as this success was, Geraint had always dreamt of the Tour de France. The biggest event in cycling, the race is notoriously tough (four cyclists have died). Geraint entered in 2007, the first Welshman to race in it since Colin Lewis in 1967.

6

Geraint – the youngest rider at just 21 – finished 140th of the 141 racers that completed the race. But even finishing the Tour de France is a huge achievement and that year 48 riders failed to. Over the following years, he improved and was a key part of the Team Sky team that helped British rider Chris Froom win the race four times.

Did you know?

The Tour de France is one of the most difficult events in sport. It began in 1903, and lasts three weeks, with the riders, who work closely together in competing teams, riding around 3,600 kilometres (2,235 miles)! Very few cyclists excel at both huge mountain climbs and long, fast flat stages. Winning the race is the ultimate dream of any cyclist!

7

In 2018, though, it was Geraint himself who won the Tour de France – the first Welshman to do so, and only the third Brit. His success was even more special because very few riders are world class in both track and road cycling. Geraint's likeable personality and his remarkable achievements over a long career make him one of Wales's most-loved athletes.

CHRIS HALLAM

The man who changed the world of disability sport

Born: Derby, 31 December 1962

Died: 16 August 2013

Sports: wheelchair racing, swimming

Swimming:

- Paralympic gold
- Paralympic silver

Wheelchair racing:

- Paralympic bronze x 2
- London Marathon wheelchair winner x 2
- World record x 2
- Great North Run wheelchair winner x 4

Other major honours:

- Disabled Sports Personality of the Year winner

1

Chris Hallam was born in England but raised in Cwmbran. An accident aged 17 could have destroyed his sporting career, but instead it made him even more determined.

He started off in the pool, and he was just days away from being selected to swim for Wales when he had a crash while travelling to training on his motorbike. Chris was paralysed below his chest.

2

Despite now needing a wheelchair, Chris didn't see why he couldn't still be an athlete. He argued that disabled children needed heroes. As soon as he left hospital, he began weightlifting and swimming sessions.

Brain and brawn

Chris didn't just train his body hard, he also used his brain. He studied other athletes' technique carefully on video and used what they did himself so that he became even better.

3

Chris had his first major success in the 50 m breaststroke, winning a gold medal in the 1984 Paralympic Games. But he became most famous for wheelchair racing. His powerful arms and shoulders, from years of swimming and weights, were a big advantage when pushing his wheelchair. In 1985 and 1987 he won the London Marathon and both times set new course records.

Pushing himself to the limit

- In 1997, Chris pushed his wheelchair over 600 miles in just 37 days, for charity.
- He did it despite having kidney failure.
- Two years later, his father saved Chris's life by giving him one of his own kidneys.

4

Chris had a fun personality and loved wearing wild outfits when competing – leopard-print lycra was his favourite! He also had flowing blond hair and he almost always wore sunglasses, earning him the nickname 'Shades'. Before this, the media had taken little notice of disability sports, but suddenly, wheelchair racing had a bright star for them to write about!

5

Chris's larger-than-life personality and medal success helped to change people's view of disability sports. Tanni-Gray Thompson (**see page 46**) said that Chris's successes in the London Marathon made wheelchair racing seem exciting.

Did you know?

In the 1990 Commonwealth Games, team officials supplied just one Wales vest for Chris and Tanni Grey-Thompson to share, as disability sport wasn't seen as important. Thankfully, disabled athletes in Wales are treated better now, and Chris and Tanni's success is a huge reason for that progress.

6

It wasn't just on the track or in the pool that Chris did great things, either. In 1986 and 1997 he rode his wheelchair all around Wales to raise money for an accessible sports centre in Cardiff and to help young racers buy wheelchairs. After retiring, he was a successful coach and a huge supporter of young disabled athletes. Sadly, Chris died aged just 50, but his legacy will always live on.

IRENE STEER

The first Welsh woman to win Olympic gold

Born: Cardiff, 10 August 1889

Died: 18 April 1977

Sport: swimming

Club: Cardiff Ladies Premier Swimming Club

Major honours include:

- Olympic gold
- British Championships gold
- Welsh Championships gold x 7
- Amateur Swimming Association gold
- Wales's first female world record holder

1

Irene Steer started swimming aged 8 in Cardiff's Roath Park Lake, and went on to be the first Welsh woman to win Olympic gold!

2

Irene loved sport from a young age and her father would take her to watch Cardiff play rugby – she later became a football fan and followed Cardiff City too. As well as swimming, she enjoyed playing water polo.

In 1907, Irene burst onto the scene by winning the Welsh Championships, and was unbeaten in that competition for seven years in a row! In 1910 she became British Champion, equalling the 100 yards (91.44m) freestyle world record.

*1 yard = 91.4 cm

Winning Welsh women

Six Welsh women have won Olympic gold:

- Irene Steer (swimming, 1912)
- Nicole Cooke (cycling, 2008)
- Jade Jones (taekwondo, 2012 and 2016)
- Elinor Barker (cycling, 2016)
- Hannah Mills (sailing, 2016 and 2020)
- Lauren Price (boxing, 2020)

Good enough for the Queen

When swimming became popular in the 1800s, it was mainly for men. But when the Queen of Sweden attended lessons with Swedish swimming instructor Nancy Edberg, women's swimming suddenly became very fashionable!

3

Irene was one of the trail-blazers of modern women's sport. It wasn't until 1912 that women were permitted to swim at the Olympics, and of the 2,500 athletes at that year's Games, just 50 were women.

Irene wanted to represent Britain in these new women's swimming events, but many doubted she'd be good enough. At just 157.5 cm tall, with small feet, Irene wasn't built like a typical swimmer. At the British trials for the 1912 Stockholm Olympics, someone said, "You don't expect to win anything with those feet, do you?"

4

Despite the doubters, she qualified and took part in the 100 m freestyle and the 4 x 100 m relay, the only two swimming events for women.

Competitive swimming in those days was very different. There weren't separate lanes for each swimmer, and during the 100 m freestyle event, Irene bumped into one of her German rivals. The Welsh wonder won the race, but was disqualified for the collision after the Germans complained.

Did you know?

The 1912 Olympic Games in Stockholm were very different to the modern Olympics. There was a tug-of-war competition, won by a team of Swedish policemen. There were also competitions for architecture, literature, music, painting and sculpture.

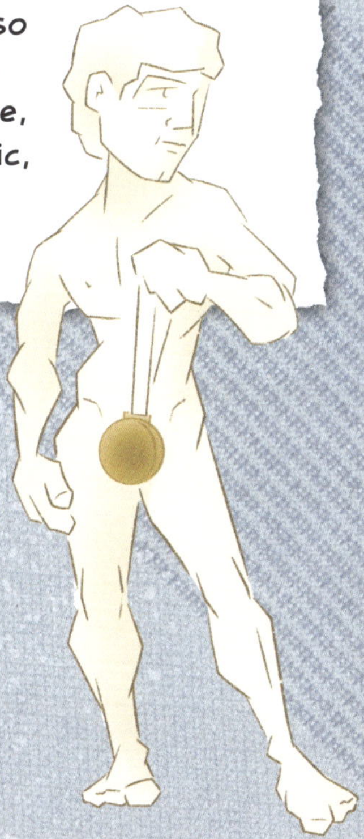

5

Thankfully, Irene won the relay event with teammates Jennie Fletcher, Belle Moore and Annie Speirs, beating Germany, Austria and Sweden in the final and breaking the world record. Today, gold medallists gleefully share their success and happiness on social media but Irene said she was very embarrassed when, after winning, they were made to walk around the pool for spectators to applaud!

6

Irene was the first and only female Welsh Olympic gold medallist until Nicole Cooke (**see page 58**) won another in 2008, 96 years later.

ALUN WYN JONES

Born: Swansea, 19 September 1985
Sport: rugby union
Position: lock, flanker
Main clubs: Swansea, Ospreys, Toulon
Wales caps: 158
Wales points: 45 (from 9 tries)
British & Irish Lions caps: 12

Major honours include:

- Most-capped international rugby player of all time (any nation)
- Grand Slam winner x 3
- Six Nations winner x 5
- Celtic League/Pro 12 winner x 3
- Anglo-Welsh Cup winner
- Six Nations Player of the Tournament
- Captain of Wales and the British & Irish Lions

The world's most-capped rugby player

1

Almost no rugby player in history from anywhere in the world has had such a long-lasting influence on his country as **Alun Wyn Jones** has had on Wales. For a remarkable 17 years, Alun was a colossal figure for both Wales and the British & Irish Lions.

Even as a boy, Alun was incredibly competitive. This would ultimately make him a star as an adult. In his youth he played with local clubs like Mumbles and Bonymaen, before coming to fame with Swansea and then the Ospreys.

If at first you don't succeed

When he first played with the Ospreys, Alun's coach said he was "dreadful". So Alun constantly analysed his game and badgered his coaches for advice on how to get better. It just shows: even the best fail sometimes.

2

Alun made his senior debut for Wales in 2006 as a flanker. But it was as a lock that he was to become an icon. Alun was a strong, athletic player and seemed to keep going forever, no matter how demanding a match was. He was famously difficult to play against and never showed any fear on the field, inspiring his teammates by always being in the thick of the action.

3

Over his long career, Alun learned what it took to be a leader by watching everyone he played with. That, combined with his obsessive will to win, saw him captain the Ospreys, Wales and the British & Irish Lions, winning three Grand Slams with Wales, three league titles with the Ospreys, and touring four times with the Lions.

4

Even in his final season, after almost two decades as a professional, Alun would still run as fast as he could between training drills, trying to get there before anyone else. His supreme effort every single day forced his teammates to try and match his standards, helping to build a winning culture.

Did you know?

- When Alun retired in 2023, Wales had played a total of 772 Test matches.
- Alun had played in 158 of them: that's 20.52%, or over $\frac{1}{5}$ of all Wales games over 142 years!
- That's a record that may never be beaten.

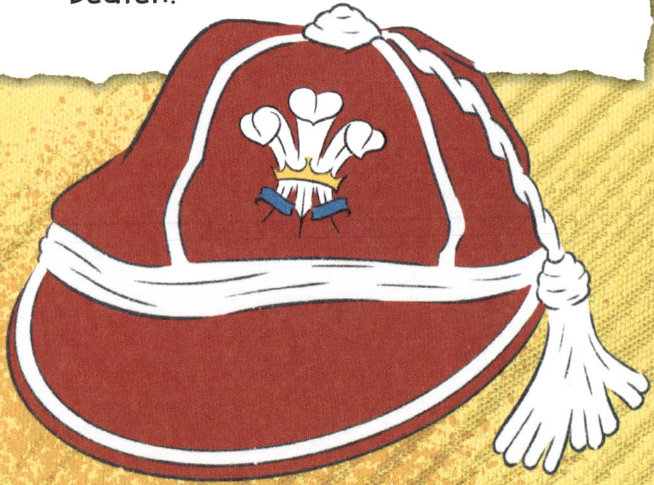

Playing the long game

In the early days of international rugby, Wales rarely played more than three games a year. If Alun had played in every Wales game from 1881 onwards, it would have taken him until 1933 to win 158 caps!

5

When he stepped down from the Wales team, moving to France to play club rugby, Alun had captained Wales 48 times. In 2023, in a 'farewell' match in Cardiff, he scored a try against Wales while playing for the all-star Barbarians.

CATH PENDLETON

1

Ice swimming is an extreme sport and involves swimming in water under 5°C, wearing only a swimsuit and a swimming cap! No wetsuits allowed. Brrrr! **Cath Pendleton** is one of the world's great ice swimmers. She was the first person ever to swim an Ice Mile in the Antarctic Polar Circle and is the Guinness World Record holder for the 'Most Southerly Ice Swim' (female).

The Merthyr Mermaid

Born: Troedyrhiw, Merthyr Tydfil, 8 March 1972

Sports: ice swimming, open water swimming

Represented: Team Great Britain

Major honours include:

- Guinness World Record holder
- World Ice Swimming Championships bronze
- First person to swim a mile inside the Antarctic Polar Circle
- First Welsh woman to swim an official Ice Mile

2

Cath, a mother of two who works for the NHS, trains for her extraordinary swims in a big freezer full of ice and water in her shed. She sits in it for up to 15 minutes around three times a week! In the winter, Cath swims in Keeper's Pond near Blaenavon up to four times a week.

3

Cath took up swimming aged 4 and loved swimming in rivers as a child. In 2013 she did her first open-water swim. Two years later she began ice swimming and by 2020 she was creating history in the Antarctic Polar Circle, where the water temperature was 0.03°C and the air temperature was −3.2°C. She spent a mind-blowing 32 minutes, 54 seconds in the water and was not allowed special swimwear to stay warm.

Don't try it yourself!

Ice and winter swimming can take place not just in the sea, but in lakes, ponds and rivers. It's a very dangerous sport and when athletes compete, they must follow strict rules and there are always medics there in case anything goes wrong.

4

If swimming in such cold water wasn't impressive enough, Cath had to wait for orca whales to get out of the way so she could begin her record-breaking attempt.

Swimming the English Channel

When she was a child, Cath promised her uncle she would swim the Channel. As an adult, she trained for it for two years and it took her 16 hours and 45 minutes to swim the 21 miles (34 km). She raised lots of money for charity!

5

That's not all Cath has achieved. She represented Great Britain at the World Ice Swimming Championships in Russia, where she won a bronze in her age category. Cath has also swum solo across the English Channel.

6

Cath jokes: "If you want to make me happy, just add cold water." She wants to be a role model for others, inspiring them to take the plunge and enjoy the thrills and health benefits of cold-water swimming.

7

Despite her incredible feats, Cath doesn't even consider herself an athlete, just someone in love with ice swimming. Most people disagree and think she is a wonderful Welsh sporting hero.

8

So next time the local pool feels a bit nippy when you dip your toe in it, think of how cold it is where Cath swims and just jump in!

Did you know?

- Humans have been swimming for thousands of years.
- 10,000-year-old cave paintings in Egypt show people doing doggy paddle!
- In India, archaeologists have found a swimming pool from 2,800 BC!

LIZA BURGESS

A rugby pioneer

Born: Newport, 24 March 1964

Sport: rugby union

Position: number 8

Main clubs: Loughborough University, Wasps, Saracens, Clifton

Wales caps: 87

Wales points: 29 (from 6 tries)*

Great Britain caps: 6

Major honours include:

- First-ever Wales Women's captain
- Played in four World Cups
- First women's domestic 'treble' winner
- Helped found Saracens Women's team
- Member of the World Rugby Hall of Fame

*Exact points aren't clear from this period in women's rugby (even Liza isn't sure), but this is the best guess!

1

Liza 'Bird' Burgess is perhaps the most important figure in the history of women's rugby in Wales. She helped establish the Wales women's team in 1987 and has been involved with it in different ways ever since.

A sporty youngster, Liza loved hockey and basketball. But her life changed forever when she first tried rugby at university. Liza had loved watching rugby but at the time there were no opportunities for young girls to play rugby in Wales. Once she got to play it, she was hooked.

No whistling on Sunday

With men's teams playing on Saturdays, it was common for women's fixtures to be on Sundays. But some strange laws existed about Sunday sport. When Liza helped found Saracens Women, she had to go to court to change an old local law saying whistles couldn't be blown on Sundays!

A team player (for both sides)

When Wales played England in 1987, there was no money for accommodation. Liza showed true sporting friendship when 12 players, Welsh and English, slept at her parents' house after the match!

2

In 1986, Liza played in the first-ever UK women's international: Great Britain against France. The players had to organise the game themselves, and the British shirts only arrived just in time for kick-off. They were too big and the players had to tape up their sleeves so they could catch the ball.

3

A year later, Wales and England formed their own teams and first played each other in Pontypool. Liza proudly captained the Dragons – something she did another 61 times! Wales lost 22-4, but Liza scored her team's only try.

4

Lots of people thought women shouldn't be playing rugby at all. It was hard for female players to access the facilities they needed and even getting enough money for kit and travel was tough.

Liza helped organise the teams she played in. In 1989 she helped persuade Saracens to launch a women's side. Saracens Women had great success and in one season they won the national league, cup and sevens tournament!

Did you know?

- The world's oldest known photo of a women's rugby team shows the Cardiff Ladies team that played Newport on 15 December 1917.
- They were raising money for soldiers in World War I.
- Most of the Cardiff players worked in a brewery and the Newport players worked for a steel company.
- One of the players later said, "We had to stop when the men came back from the war, which was a shame. Such great fun we had."

5

In 1991, Liza captained Wales in the first-ever women's World Cup. She played for Wales for 20 years, and after retiring as a player, coached Wales at age grade and senior levels.

6

In 2018, Liza was named in the prestigious World Rugby Hall of Fame. It was the first time a Welsh woman had achieved this.

JIMMY WILDE

The 'Ghost with a Hammer in his Hand'

Born: Quakers Yard, Merthyr Tydfil, 15 May 1892

Died: 10 March 1969

Sport: boxing

Weight: flyweight, bantamweight

Professional record: 132 wins, 4 losses, 1 draw*

Major honours include:

- World Flyweight Champion
- European Flyweight Champion
- British Flyweight Champion
- Welsh Sports Hall of Fame
- *Ring* magazine Hall of Fame
- International Boxing Hall of Fame

*Exact fighting statistics aren't clear from this period, but this is the best guess!

1

William James Wilde was just 157 cm tall, but he towers over the history of Welsh, British and even world boxing. Nicknamed 'The Mighty Atom', 'The Tylorstown Terror' and the 'Ghost with the Hammer in his Hand', he is considered the greatest flyweight (weighing 49–51 kg) boxer ever. Despite his incredible power, he never weighed more than 49 kg, and legend has it that he sometimes got weighed in for fights with rocks in his pockets to add to his weight so he was allowed to fight.

A hall of fame fighter

- The International Boxing Hall of Fame (IBHOF) was founded in New York in 1990.
- Jimmy was one of the very first fighters honoured, along with superstars like Muhammad Ali, Joe Louis and Joe Frazier.
- In 1992, Jimmy was inducted into the Welsh Sports Hall of Fame.

2

As a child, Jimmy worked in a coal mine like his dad. He could work in tight spots others couldn't fit into, but he suffered a serious leg injury aged 15 and couldn't work for a year. It also made it hard for him to join the Army in the First World War, but he kept trying and was eventually accepted as a PE instructor.

A powerful punch

Today, boxing writers and historians still consider Jimmy one of the greatest punchers ever. His technique, timing and power allowed him to hit far harder than other men of his size. The respected boxing magazine *Ring* judged him the third-greatest puncher in boxing history.

3

Before becoming a professional, Jimmy fought in fairground booths against any challenger who fancied their chances. He could apparently knock out men twice his weight, despite his skinny physique. Sometimes he had 25 fights in one evening!

4

He won 132 of his professional fights – 98 by knockout – and only lost four times. Jimmy claimed that including his fairground fights, he fought over 800 times! Boxers back then fought constantly, unlike today, and it was very bad for their body and mind. Once Jimmy fought two professional fights in one day and won both of them by knockout! He was victorious in 103 professional contests before he ever lost, the third longest unbeaten streak in boxing.

5

In 1916, Jimmy became the first official World Flyweight Champion, and he also won lots of British and European titles. His career was so impressive that he was inducted into the prestigious International Boxing Hall of Fame. Sadly, despite his success, he spent his later years in poverty. He died aged 76, never recovering from a mugging four years earlier.

Did you know?

As far back as the early 18th century, travelling fairs held boxing contests, where you could challenge pros to win prizes. It's probably better to stick to candy floss and the dodgems!

6

Jimmy is easily one of the most globally respected Welsh athletes, and is still often included in the Top Ten greatest boxers of all time.

JOHN CHARLES

Born: Cwmbwrla, Swansea, 27 December 1931

Died: 21 February 2004

Sport: football

Position: centre forward, centre back

Main clubs: Swansea Town (Youth), Leeds United, Juventus, Roma, Cardiff City, Hereford United, Merthyr Tydfil

Club goals: 370

Wales caps: 38

Wales goals: 15

Teams managed: Hereford United, Merthyr Tydfil, Hamilton Steelers

Major honours include:

- Serie A title winner x 3
- Italian Cup winner x 2
- Ballon d'Or 3rd place (highest-ever Welsh player)
- Football Hall of Fame
- Welsh Sports Hall of Fame
- In 2003 voted the most outstanding Welsh player of the past 50 years

The Gentle Giant

1

John Charles is one of Wales's greatest sportsmen. His name still inspires adoration around the footballing world – especially in Italy, where he excelled for Juventus.

2

His career began at Swansea Town, but he moved to Leeds United after a scout saw him playing football in the park. At first John played in defence, but after being shifted to centre forward, his phenomenal pace, power, ball control and heading ability made him a regular scorer. At 18, John was capped for Wales. He captained Leeds, got them promoted and scored 157 goals in his time there, from 1949 to 1957. John is still the club's second highest scorer of all time.

Building a legacy

- In 1956, fire destroyed Leeds United's West Stand.
- The money from John's transfer to Juventus was used to rebuild it.
- When he died, it was renamed the 'John Charles Stand'.

3

But the biggest moment was his record-breaking 1957 transfer to Juventus, the 'aristocrats' of Italian football. British players moving to Italy was rare then, but he embraced the lifestyle and language and became a hero there. Playing upfront and in defence, he helped Juventus win three league titles and two cup titles, slamming home 95 goals! In his first season, he was voted Player of the Season and was the highest goalscorer in the league.

4

John was a fanatical trainer and usually the last to leave each day. His workouts could be unusual: he perfected his leaping ability by jumping up to head the crossbar!

5

In Italy, fans called him *Il Gigante Buono* (The Gentle Giant). He was celebrated for never losing his temper on the field, even when opponents did things that would get you sent off now! The Welsh giant never received a yellow or red card in his career. It was once said that if everyone played as fairly as him, you wouldn't need referees.

Did you know?

John played in the 1958 World Cup with his younger brother, Mel, who won 31 caps for Wales. It was the last time Wales played in the tournament until 2022.

Loved in Italy

In 1997, Italian football fans voted John the best foreign player ever to have played in Italy. Considering he left Italy 34 years earlier, this was impressive!

6

John won 38 caps for Wales, scoring 15 goals, and playing in the 1958 World Cup. Unfortunately, the Hungarian team purposely injured him and he couldn't play in the next match against Brazil. Many feel this cost Wales their chance to progress. He went on to play for Roma, Cardiff City, Hereford United and Merthyr Tydfil before retiring to Leeds.

7

The great football manager Sir Bobby Robson said, "John wasn't only one of the greatest footballers who ever lived. He was one of the greatest men ever to play the game."

COLIN JACKSON

Hurdling to glory

Born: Cardiff, 18 February 1967

Sport: athletics (hurdling, sprinting)

Club: Brecon Athletics Club

Major honours include:

- Olympic silver
- World Championships gold x 2
- World Indoor Championships gold
- European Championships gold x 4
- European Indoor Championships gold x 4
- Commonwealth Games gold x 2
- World record holder
- BBC Cymru Wales Sports Personality of the Year x 3

1

Colin Jackson is one of the most celebrated figures in Welsh and British athletics, winning a host of medals at major tournaments, competing in 110 m hurdles, 60 m hurdles and the 4 x 100 m relay.

2

Born in Cardiff in 1967, Colin is from a Jamaican family. He was a keen cricketer in his youth and captained his school side, but at 13 was not selected for the Welsh national cricket team for his age group. Colin believes this was due to racism. Cricket's loss was athletics' gain.

3

At first Colin tried the decathlon (where you compete in ten different track and field events), before switching to the high hurdles. It paid off. Aged just 21, Colin won a silver medal at the 1988 Seoul Olympics. He went on to become a four-time European Champion, double Commonwealth Champion and double World Champion. Colin also became the first British athlete to regain a world title after losing it, and was a world record holder for 13 years at 110 m, and 27 years at 60 m.

4

Colin broke multiple world, European, British and Commonwealth records. A lightning-fast starter, he also won many tight contests thanks to his famous ability to dip for the finish line. From 1993 to 1995, Colin won 44 consecutive races! He was simply unstoppable!

Discriminating against dragons?

Colin believes that sometimes British selectors discriminated against him for being Welsh. He said, "I was number one or two in the country and they... seemed to have that little bit of favouritism to the English runners."

5

Sadly, Olympic gold escaped Colin. He was tipped for gold in 1992 and breezed through his first heat, but picked up an injury after not warming up properly and finished seventh in the final. Frustratingly, his time in the first heat was faster than the gold medallist's time in the final.

6

Many consider him one of the greatest athletes ever not to have won Olympic gold. After retiring, Colin has worked as a coach and broadcaster. In 2005 he finished second on *Strictly Come Dancing* and in 2021 he finished third in *Dancing on Ice*.

Did you know?

Hurdling probably began in England in the early 19th century. The modern hurdle was invented in 1935. It's designed to fall safely if an athlete knocks it over, avoiding injuries.

Jumping all over the world

Below is a list of some of the cities where Colin won medals. Do you know which country each one is in?

Edinburgh
Rome
Athens
Budapest
Maebashi
Paris
Munich
The Hague
Auckland
Manchester
Helsinki
Seoul
Liévin
Stuttgart
Toronto

NON EVANS

Wales's multi-talented wonder

1

Non Evans is one of the greatest all-round athletes Wales has ever produced. Some know her best as a rugby star, some as a weightlifter or powerlifter, others as a judo or wrestling expert.

2

She was a bundle of energy from the very start, walking at just 9 months and running soon after. Her first success came in judo, which she started aged 10. In her teens, she won Welsh and British titles and silver at the Commonwealth Judo Championships.

3 At university, Non started rugby and was soon playing for Wales. She somehow found time to win a world youth title in powerlifting too!

Born: Swansea, 20 June 1974

Sports: rugby union, judo, weightlifting, freestyle wrestling, powerlifting

Rugby position: full back, wing, centre

Wales rugby caps: 87

Wales points: 489 (including 64 tries)

Judo:
- Commonwealth Judo Championships silver x 2

Weightlifting:
- Welsh Weightlifting Championships gold
- British Weightlifting Championships gold

Wrestling:
- Welsh Wrestling Championships gold
- British Wrestling Championships silver

Powerlifting:
- World Youth Powerlifting Championships gold

Other honours include:
- First woman to compete in three different sports at the Commonwealth Games
- Selected for rugby World XV team

4 Non then switched to weightlifting and became both a Welsh and British champion. She competed in two different sports in the same Commonwealth Games: judo and wrestling. This was both impressive and dangerous, as Non had to be different weights to compete in different events on consecutive days.

No regrets

Non couldn't be a professional rugby player: the Welsh Rugby Union didn't put the women's team on full-time contracts until 2022. But Non is happy this gave her the opportunity to do other sports.

5

Rugby, however, is the sport Non is most known for. She won 87 caps and scored an astonishing 64 tries for Wales – the most of any Welsh player, male or female. She was at one point the highest scorer in women's international rugby. Non's most famous moment came in 2009 when she kicked a last-minute match-winning penalty for Wales to beat England for the first time ever in women's rugby. Non played in two women's Rugby World Cups – one after breaking her leg so badly that doctors told her she'd never run again.

6

Non also took up wrestling, and in 2010, she was in both the Rugby World Cup and the Welsh wrestling team for the Commonwealth Games! This made her the first woman to compete in the Commonwealth Games in three different sports.

7

Most impressively, Non achieved all these things as an amateur, always having to work full time to support her sporting life.

Did you know?

- Wrestling is one of the oldest forms of combat sport.
- There is evidence of women wrestling in 330 BC!
- Cave paintings of wrestling have been found in France – they're 15,000 years old!

Rugby history

Before Non kicked the penalty that defeated England in 2009, Wales Women had played their rival 24 times and lost every time. At the time of publication, they have won just twice in 41 matches against the Red Roses.

8

After rugby, Non continued to succeed at new challenges, becoming the first female rugby presenter on S4C, commentating at the Olympics, and appearing on TV's *Gladiators*! Non received an MBE in 2011, the first female rugby player to be awarded the honour.

WILF WOOLLER

Wales's greatest all-round male athlete

Born: Rhos-on-Sea, 20 November 1912

Died: 10 March 1997

Sports: cricket, rugby, squash, football

Cricket clubs: Denbighshire, Cambridge University, Glamorgan, Marylebone

- Captained Glamorgan for 14 years
- County Championship winner
- England cricket selector

Main rugby clubs: Colwyn Bay, Sale, Cambridge University, Cardiff

Position: centre, wing

Wales caps: 18

Wales points: 26 (including 6 tries)

- Captained Wales
- Beat the All Blacks

Football clubs: Cardiff City, Barry Town

Squash: represented Wales

1

Wilfred Wooller excelled at many sports, despite losing several years of his sporting career to the Second World War, much of it as a prisoner of war in Singapore.

2

Wilf played centre and wing in his rugby career and made his Wales debut aged just 20 in 1933. He made an amazing late try-saving tackle to secure Wales's first-ever victory over England at Twickenham. He also played in the 1935 team that defeated the All Blacks – one of only three Wales teams ever to beat New Zealand.

3

Wilf captained his nation four times and was famed for his huge kick, running skills and excellent ball control. Wilf was a giant for the era at 188 cm, yet was still very fast. For Cardiff, he scored 204 points in 71 games.

4

Wilf also once scored a hat-trick for Cardiff City at football, and played for Barry Town too. He represented Cambridge University at both cricket and rugby, a sign of his varied talents.

14-man Wales beat New Zealand

When Wales played the All Blacks in 1935, their hooker Don Tarr broke his neck early in the second half and no replacements were allowed back then. Losing 12-10 with minutes to go, Wilf made a break and kicked ahead, setting up the winning try.

Political views

For a long time, South Africa were banned from international sport because their government implemented a cruel system known as apartheid, which discriminated against non-white people. Wilf, however, was a supporter of South African sport, making him quite unpopular.

5

During the Second World War, Wilf was captured by the Japanese. Prisoners had to do dangerous manual labour with very little food, and many died. Wilf was so physically changed, it ended his rugby career.

6

Instead, he became famous for cricket, playing for Glamorgan for 24 years. In 1948, he led them to their first County Championship title (one of only three they've ever won). This win was a huge shock as older cricket clubs saw Glamorgan as inferior.

7

A strong bowler and fierce batter, Wilf's intense will to win didn't make him very popular with opposing players and fans. He was selected twice to play for England*, but both times he couldn't accept because of work. He would later become a selector for England, and served as Secretary for Glamorgan for 30 years and as President for six years.

*which represents England and Wales

8

Incredibly, Wilf also found time to represent Wales at squash and was later a handy bowls player. He also worked as a top journalist and broadcaster. He truly lived an extraordinary life!

Did you know?

- The Japanese forced Wilf to help build the Burma Railway.
- Up to 270,000 civilians and 60,000 prisoners of war worked on it.
- Around 90,000 civilians and 12,000 prisoners died.

TANNI GREY-THOMPSON

From 'Tiny' beginnings to enormous feats

Born: Cardiff, 26 July 1969

Sport: wheelchair racing

Major honours include:

- 16 medals at the Paralympic Games (including 11 gold)
- 12 World Championship medals (including 5 gold)
- London Wheelchair Marathon winner x 6
- Broke 30 world records
- Member of the Gorsedd at the National Eisteddfod
- Peerage in the House of Lords
- BBC Wales Sports Personality of the Year x 3
- BBC Sports Personality of the Year Lifetime Achievement Award

1

When **Carys Davina Grey-Thompson** was born, her two-year-old sister nicknamed her 'Tiny', which became 'Tanni'. Tanni was born with spina bifida, which damaged her spinal cord and nerves. Although at first she was able to walk, by the age of 7 she needed a wheelchair.

2

Tanni's parents encouraged her to do sport. She learned to jump kerbs and steps in her wheelchair when she went out with friends and developed incredible strength and physical control.

3 She was inspired to take up wheelchair racing at age 13, and when she saw Chris Hallam win the London Marathon (**see page 16**), she vowed to take part. While many may have thought this was a crazy dream, she didn't. Tanni didn't just achieve her dream of competing in the marathon, she won it an amazing six times! In her youth, she also played wheelchair basketball.

Did you know?

- Wheelchair racing has officially been part of the Paralympics since 1964.
- Elite racers can reach speeds of 40 km/h (24.9 mph)!
- The wheelchairs are built for the individual needs of each racer and cost thousands of pounds.

4 Tanni kept having to overcome further complications. At 17 she underwent major surgery to have a metal rod grafted onto her spine. Not even this stopped her.

5

Tanni's hard work and powerful will saw her break a stunning 30 world records and win an astonishing 16 medals in five Paralympic Games between 1988 and 2004, plus 12 World Championship medals. Her medals came for distances from 100 metres to 800 metres and her repeated success in the London Marathon showed her versatility. In 2002 she won the London Wheelchair Marathon just three months after giving birth.

What are the Paralympic Games?

- The Paralympics began in 1948, when the Olympic Games were in London. 16 disabled war veterans competed.
- Today, the Paralympics involve almost 4,500 athletes from around the world.
- The Summer version has 22 sports and the Winter version six sports, each with multiple categories aligned to the abilities of the athletes.

6

Tanni was named BBC Wales Sports Personality of the Year three times. Since retiring, she has had a hugely successful career in the media and in politics, where she works on law-making in the House of Lords, and she passionately champions sport. Tanni is, without doubt, one of the most inspirational figures in Welsh sporting history.

What does T53 mean?

Tanni competed in the T53 classification in wheelchair racing, for athletes who have full use of their arms, but limited or no use of their abdomen or legs. Tanni is one of the most famous and respected athletes ever to compete in this category.

STEVE ROBINSON

From shelf-stacker to world champion

Born: Cardiff, 13 December 1968

Sport: boxing

Weight: featherweight, super featherweight

Professional record: 32 wins (17 by knockout), 17 losses, 2 draws

Major honours include:

- World Featherweight champion
- Intercontinental Featherweight champion
- European Featherweight champion
- Welsh Area Featherweight champion

1

If you like sport and surprise endings, you'll love the story of **Steve Robinson**. This Welsh boxer has such a remarkable tale that his nickname is 'The Cinderella Man'.

2

Born in Ely in Cardiff in 1968, Steve was a sports-mad child, bursting with energy. His small size and skin colour led to him being bullied. But he learned to look after himself after joining a boxing gym.

Despite being a natural, Steve gave up fighting as a teenager. He left school and was struggling to find work when he bumped into his old boxing coach, who said Steve had the talent to be a world champion. Steve went back to the gym and soon went professional.

3

His early career wasn't glamorous. By March 1993, of Steve's 23 fights, he'd won just 13. He didn't earn much from boxing and had to stack shelves in a department store.

4

Then something extraordinary happened. Colombian Rubén Palacio was due to fight Englishman John Davison to defend his world featherweight title. But Palacio had a serious health issue and couldn't fight. His title was now up for grabs, and organisers had just days to find an opponent for Davison. Boxers train for months before a big fight and nobody wanted to fight at such short notice. Eventually, with almost no one left to ask, they approached Steve.

He was eating pie and chips when he got a call saying he had two days to get ready for a world title fight. And to compete at featherweight level, he had to lose about 3.6 kg!

A proud champion

Steve was the first black Welsh world boxing champion. Growing up in a one-parent family, life was tough. Today, Steve campaigns for facilities for young people from disadvantaged backgrounds.

5

For two days, he trained intensively, wearing lots of clothes to help sweat weight out. It was exhausting, but it worked. The problem was that on the day of the fight, he was hungry and tired. No one thought this weary, almost unknown fighter had a chance.

6

Yet Steve shocked the world. Not only did he start well, he got better the longer the fight went on, and won a decision from the judges. The shelf-stacker was now world champion! He proved it was no fluke by defending his title seven times.

7

Steve's story is a great example of always believing in yourself, working hard and making the most of any opportunities that come your way.

Dragons on top of the world

Wales has produced 14 world champion boxers. First was flyweight Percy Jones from Porth, who won his title in 1914, then Freddie Welsh and Jimmy Wilde (**see page 31**). The others are Howard Winstone, Steve Robinson, Robbie Regan, Barry Jones, Joe Calzaghe, Enzo Maccarinelli, Gavin Rees, Nathan Cleverly, Lee Selby, Joe Cordina and Lauren Price (**see page 10**).

Did you know?

- Boxing was in the original Olympics from 688 BC.
- Art from around 1350 BC in Thebes, Egypt shows boxers competing for spectators.
- The earliest art showing boxers with gloves, rather than bare fists, comes from Crete in 1500 BC.

JADE JONES

The 'Headhunter'

Born: Bodelwyddan, 21 March 1993

Sport: taekwondo

Major honours include:

- Olympic gold x 2
- World Championships gold
- Commonwealth Games gold
- Grand Prix event gold x 10
- European Games gold x 2
- European Championships gold x 3
- Youth Olympic Games gold
- BBC Wales Sports Personality of the Year x 2

1

Jade Jones had an unusual start in the sport she became an Olympic and world champion in. Aged 8, Jade often misbehaved and her grandad sent her to the local taekwondo club to channel her energy. And, wow, did it work!

2

Jade fell for the sport straight away and was desperate to learn. She finished school aged 16 to take it up full time. Taekwondo is a martial art where fighters punch and kick each other and Jade, who liked to aim high with her kicks to score more points, soon earned the nickname 'The Headhunter'.

Covid warriors

During Covid lockdowns, Jade couldn't train with her coaches at the gym. So she and her housemate Bianca Walkden (a three-time taekwondo world champion) transformed their garage into a gym so they could still train intensively every day.

3

There isn't a lot of money in taekwondo and Jade had to work hard to get the funding to compete. She travelled to Singapore for the Summer Youth Olympic Games thanks to donations from businesses in her local town, Flint.

She repaid them by winning gold. It was one of many medals she collected before heading to the London Olympics in 2012, aged just 19.

4

Jade trained incredibly hard, spending five hours a day sparring and weight training and countless more analysing videos of her opponents. It paid off, as she battled to gold in the 57 kg weight class. In the semi-final Jade beat the world number one fighter and in the final beat the world champion, despite suffering two painful knocks early in the fight. She was the first British fighter to win gold in taekwondo, and is one of only three Welsh women ever to have won a solo Olympic gold.

5

Jade was favourite to retain her title in the 2016 Olympics in Rio, Brazil, putting new pressure on her. She admitted to crying with nerves before the semi-final. But she kept her title and became the first Welsh athlete to win back-to-back Olympic gold in any individual event.

6

Jade is a huge believer in what sports can do for people, saying, "Getting involved in sports sets young people down the right path. Life can be tough, and training gives you the drive and discipline you need to succeed."

As for Jade's gold medals, her grandad looks after them. While he's thrilled with the result of sending his granddaughter to taekwondo, he still doesn't trust her not to lose them!

The secret ingredient to success

Elite athletes' nutritionists make sure they eat the right food so they're in tip-top shape. But that doesn't mean they can't sometimes have what they love. Jade admits that one of the secrets to her success is pasta and jelly before her bouts!

7

In 2025, Jade announced she is taking up boxing. She's dreaming of being a world champion in that sport too!

Did you know?

- Taekwondo was created in the 1940s and 1950s.
- Fighters mixed traditional Korean martial arts with fighting styles from China and Japan.
- Taekwondo can be translated as 'the art of kicking and punching'.

ARTHUR GOULD

Rugby's first superstar

Born: Newport, 10 October 1864

Died: 2 January 1919

Sport: rugby union

Position: centre, full back

Main clubs: Newport, London Welsh, Richmond

Wales caps: 27

Wales points: 13 (including 4 tries)

Major honours include:

- Led Wales to their first Championship and Triple Crown
- Captained Wales 18 times
- Broke the record for most national caps in world rugby
- Welsh Sports Hall of Fame
- World Rugby Hall of Fame

1

Arthur 'Monkey' Gould was not just Welsh rugby's first superstar, but world rugby's. He helped to make Wales a serious force and raised the profile of the game inside and outside the country.

2

Arthur got his nickname as a boy, thanks to his tree-climbing – a skill he used in a match against England, when he shimmied up the rugby posts to fix the crossbar! A centre and full back, while still a teenager he played for Newport, a major club at the time. After scoring two tries on his debut, he was never dropped. In that first game the captain called him a 'devil', as he ignored the skipper's pleas to kick and ran instead. Another great Welsh player, Gwyn Nicholls, said trying to tackle him was like trying to "catch a butterfly in flight with a hat pin".

Earning an income

As rugby was amateur, Arthur had to work full time too. He also sometimes entered athletics competitions to win money. A fantastic sprinter and hurdler, he won over £1,000 – a fortune then.

3

Arthur could kick with both feet, had a deadly sidestep and loved being the centre of attention. His image was used to sell everything from chocolate to cigarettes.

4

He won 27 caps, a remarkable total in an era when Wales averaged three games a year. Nobody won more caps as a centre for Wales until 1980. For 18 of his Test matches, Arthur was captain – a Welsh record until 1994, when Wales regularly played more than ten games a season.

5

In 1890, Arthur led his country to their first win over England. He also took Wales to their first-ever Triple Crown in 1893 – the biggest prize in European rugby at the time.

6

In 1896, an adoring public raised hundreds of pounds to buy him a house! Rugby was strictly amateur then and the British rugby community was so angry about this that the Welsh Rugby Union had to leave the International Rugby Football Board. Scotland and Ireland even cancelled fixtures with Wales. To end the dispute, Arthur announced his retirement from international rugby.

A talented family

Arthur had five brothers:

- They all played for Newport, one of the best British teams at the time.
- Bert won 3 Wales caps and played in the 1893 Triple Crown.
- Bob won 11 Wales caps and played 136 times for Newport.
- Wyatt ran the 400 m hurdles in the 1908 Olympics.

7

Arthur retired just before Wales's first Golden Era, but was credited with laying the foundations for Wales becoming the best side in the world from 1900 to 1911.

Did you know?

When Arthur started playing for Wales, there were no points in rugby! Amazingly, one converted try or drop goal beat ANY number of unconverted tries, so you could score five tries and lose to one drop goal! Points were introduced in the 1890/91 season.

NICOLE COOKE

The Wick Wonder

Born: Swansea, 13 April 1983

Sport: cycling (road)

Club: Cardiff Ajax CC

Major honours include:

- Olympic gold
- World Championships gold
- Commonwealth gold
- British National Road Race gold x 10
- Tour de France winner x 2
- UCI Women's Road World Cup x 2
- Giro d'Italia winner
- Tour of Flanders winner
- First British cyclist (male or female) to win a Grand Tour
- BBC Wales Sports Personality of the Year

1

Nicole Cooke grew up in Wick, in the Vale of Glamorgan. She was obsessed with bikes from a young age, taking part in everything from track racing to mountain biking and hill climbing. She even made cycling to school part of her training and dreamed of winning the Tour de France.

2 At 16, Nicole competed against adults in the women's British National Road Race Championship. Unbelievably, she triumphed, after winning a dramatic contest with a former world record holder!

A treasure in the attic

As a child, Nicole found an old tandem bike in her attic. Her dad, who had been a cyclist in his youth, restored it and got another and the whole family began taking cycling holidays together. Nicole was hooked!

3 The victory marked the start of a glittering career in which she not only won the Tour de France, she won it twice.

4 Being a woman cyclist from Wales wasn't easy. She taught herself about tactics by watching racing on television, searching the internet and talking to women who had raced on roads. She even learned Italian and moved to Italy aged 18 so she could compete at the highest level. It worked: that year she won gold in the Commonwealth Games.

The women's Tour de France

- The first-ever Tour de France took place in 1903.
- The first women's event wasn't until 1955.
- The second women's event wasn't until 1984!

5

The following year, Nicole won four World Cup races on the trot, becoming the youngest winner of the World Cup Series. But she had multiple serious injuries, and was often frustrated with the lack of support female cyclists got in Wales. Welsh officials sent Nicole to defend her Commonwealth title with no teammates for her race, while there was a team of six for the men's race, none of whom even finished. Alone, Nicole lost to a team of six Australians.

Did you know?

In the nineteenth century, in the early days of cycling, it was incorrectly believed that it would seriously damage women's health. It was also very difficult for women to cycle in the long dresses they had to wear.

6

Nicole's greatest achievement was becoming the first racer (male or female) to win the World Championship Road Race and Olympic gold in the same year. Her gold at the 2008 Beijing Olympics was the first cycling gold ever won by a British woman. She was also the first Welsh woman to win an individual Olympic gold and the first Welsh woman to win gold since Irene Steer in 1912 (**see page 19**).

7

Nicole retired at 29, angry that rivals using performance-enhancing drugs had robbed her of several titles. She wrote an autobiography which was nominated for several awards, and was praised for highlighting the extra difficulties women in cycling face compared to men.

BILLY BOSTON

The star who had to leave Wales to shine

Born: Cardiff, 6 August 1934

Sports: rugby league, rugby union

Position: wing, centre

Main clubs: CIACs, Neath, Pontypridd (rugby union); Wigan, Blackpool Boro (rugby league)

Great Britain caps (rugby league): 32

GB points: 75 (from 25 tries)

Major honours include:

- Rugby League World Cup winner
- Rugby League Challenge Cup winner x 3
- League Championship winner
- British Rugby League Hall of Fame
- Welsh Sports Hall of Fame
- Rugby Football League Hall of Fame
- Record try-scorer with Wigan (478)

1

Billy Boston is one of the greatest rugby league players of all time. He was a living legend in England during his playing days, but for many years his brilliance wasn't recognised in Wales.

Record breaker

Billy's amazing try-scoring record of 571 tries is impressive not only because it's the second-highest individual total ever – he also achieved it in just 564 matches!

Did you know?

- From 1895 to 1995, you couldn't receive any money for playing rugby union.
- During this time, around one in four Welsh international players left to play rugby league.
- This stopped them from representing Wales in rugby union ever again.

2

Billy was born in Cardiff, one of 11 children. His family was from Wales, Ireland and Sierra Leone (West Africa). He played rugby union with Cardiff Schoolboys and Wales Youth and began his senior rugby with the CIACS club in Cardiff. He was famed for his speed, athleticism and try-scoring ability. His dream was to play for Cardiff and Wales.

3

Despite his excellence, Cardiff never approached him. So when other clubs like Neath and Pontypridd showed interest, he joined them. Similarly, Billy was never picked to play for Wales. Many believe it was because he wasn't white.

4

When Billy was just 18, Wigan – one of the top professional rugby league teams – signed him for an enormous sum. In those days, turning professional meant Billy would never be able to play rugby union again.

5

Billy may not have dreamed of playing rugby league, but he had a dream career. He became one of the greatest players of all time. His pace, agility, power and footwork dazzled both opponents and fans. He scored a massive 478 tries in 488 matches for Wigan, a record that is likely never to be broken.

Keeping his mum's word

Wigan offered Billy £1,500 to sign for them, but Billy didn't want to leave Wales. His mother wanted to get rid of the Wigan officials, so she told them he'd only sign for double that. They instantly agreed to a fee of £3,000 – a fortune at that time. Billy didn't want to sign as turning professional meant he could never play for Cardiff or Wales, but he kept his mother's promise.

6

Billy was selected for Great Britain in rugby league after just six club games – the first black player to represent them. He scored a record 36 tries* in 18 games on his first tour. He played 32 times for Great Britain and helped them win the 1960 World Cup.

*Some of these tries were not against international teams, so they don't count in official statistics.

7

In recent years, Billy's achievements have been recognised more in Wales. A statue of him was put up in Cardiff Bay in 2023 and there are two others, in Wigan and at Wembley in London. He was also knighted in 2025!

JESS FISHLOCK

Wales's most-capped footballer

Born: Cardiff, 14 January 1987

Sport: football

Position: midfielder

Main clubs: Cardiff City, Bristol Academy, Melbourne Victory (Australia), FFC Frankfurt (Germany), OL Reign (USA)

Wales caps: 165 (as of July 2025)

Wales goals: 48 (as of July 2025)

Major honours include:

- Welsh Footballer of the Year x 5
- Multiple championship titles and cup wins in Australia, USA, Scotland, France and the Netherlands
- UEFA Champions League winner
- First player (male or female) to win 100+ caps for Wales
- Wales's all-time top goalscorer (male or female)
- US National Women's Soccer League Most Valuable Player winner

1

No footballer, man or woman, has played so many times for Wales as the incredible **Jess Fishlock**, one of the best midfielders in world football. She fell in love with the sport aged 7, when she went along to keep her sister company at a football camp and became obsessed with the sport.

2

When Jess was young, there were few opportunities for women to earn a living playing football, or even to get quality coaching or play with other world-class players.

Women, war, Wales and football

Women's football became popular during World War I, when men were away fighting. Women's matches raised money for the war effort. Sadly, in 1922 the Football Association of Wales banned women from playing at member clubs, killing off women's football until the ban was lifted in the 1970s.

3

Jess made her debut for Cardiff City Ladies at 15 and the Wales Under-19 side at 16. In one of her early matches for the senior team, Jess impressed the opposition so much she was offered her first professional contract with AZ Alkmaar in the Netherlands.

The trailblazers of women's football in Wales

- Wales Women's unofficial first match was in 1973. They lost to Ireland.
- The official national women's team was established in 1993.
- Jess helped Wales women qualify for Euro 2025 – their first major tournament.

4

It was a dream come true for Jess, but it was hard. Despite feeling terribly homesick, she stuck at it and succeeded, helping AZ Alkmaar win two league titles.

5

Jess has also won praise for speaking about her struggles as a gay athlete. In 2018 she was awarded an MBE for services to football and the LGBTQ+ community.

6

Jess has played most of her football in America, home to the best women's teams in the world for many years. She has also played in France, England, Australia, Scotland and Germany. But no matter where she is in the world, she always answers the call to play for Wales, and is their most-capped player ever – male or female. She has captained Wales on many occasions and scored some of their most important and impressive goals. Jess scored for Wales in the 2025 Euros. At 38 years old, she became the oldest goalscorer in the tournament's history.

Did you know?

Today, women's football is a huge global sport and millions of girls and women around the world watch, play and support it. The number of UK women and girls playing football has increased by 56% since 2020, and 77% of schools now offer equal access for girls to play.

Activities

1 Which Welsh sporting hero in this book do you think is the greatest athlete of all? Why?

2 Have you ever seen any of the stars in this book competing?

3 Draw a picture of your favourite athlete and put it on the wall.

4 What story or event in this book most shocked you? Did anything the heroes went through sound really terrible?

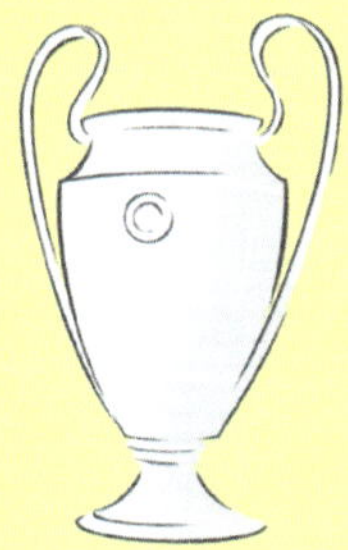

5 Write a short story about what it must have been like to play rugby in the nineteenth century. Do you think it would be more or less fun than playing today? Why?

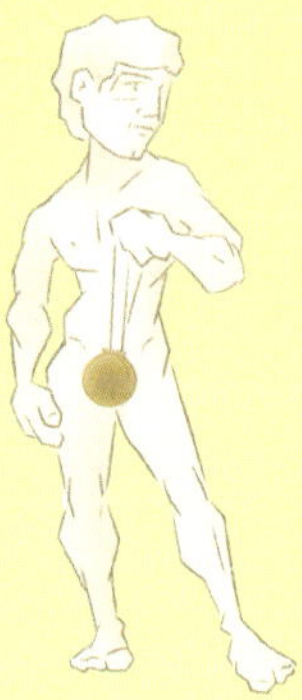

6 Are there any Welsh sporting heroes you think should have been in this book that aren't here? Write your own chapters about them.

7 Pick your Welsh 'Dream Team'. Select three men and women from this book and draw them in your own special Team Wales kit.

8 Invent a chapter about your future sporting career and draw a picture of yourself.

9 What would you like to be? A rugby star? A wheelchair champion? A football hero? An amazing cyclist? Why?

10 Which story in here inspired you the most? Why?

11 The athletes in this book do all sorts of crazy and intense training. Which training would you like to do and which training would be your worst nightmare, and why?

12 Ask your teacher, parents or family who their Welsh sporting hero is, and why. Are they in this book?

My sporting hero

Do some research online and fill in this factfile about your favourite sportsperson. Then stick in a photo or draw a picture of them in the box.

Name: ....

Born: (where?) ....

.... (date?) ....

Sport: ....

Position: ....

Clubs: ....

....

National caps: ....

Points/Goals: ....

Major honours include:

....

....

....

....

....

....

....

Your wonderful sporting profile

Create your own sporting profile. Write down the things you'd love to achieve in your favourite sport and imagine all the honours you'd like to win. Once you've done that, draw a picture of yourself to go along with it. Who knows, perhaps you'll make it all come true one day!

Name: ....

Born: (where?) ....

.... (date?) ....

Sport: ....

Position: ....

Clubs: ....

....

National caps: ....

Points/Goals: ....

Major honours include:

....

....

....

....

....

....

....

Acknowledgements

I would like to thank my editor Carolyn Hodges for all her hard work on this book and for the passion she put into every page. It's always a huge pleasure to work with her and I hope we get many more opportunities to do so. I appreciate the efforts of everyone at Y Lolfa who helped me to get these amazing Welsh stories out there and into the hands of children – in particular Lefi Gruffudd, Richard Huw Pritchard and Teleri Haf Jones.

Thanks to Telor Gwyn for his unique illustrations. I must also give a special mention to Steve Hunt, Jon Newcombe, Huw Richards and Miles Templeton for helping me clarify a few obscure (and much disputed) sporting stats.

Finally, thanks to my wife, Helena, and my children, Michael and Heli, for being so tolerant of all the long hours I have spent sitting at my desk writing about amazing athletes from my faraway homeland! Michael and Heli, I hope these tales bring you a little closer to the Land of Your Fathers.

James Stafford
Prague, September 2025

www.jpstafford.com

From the same author:

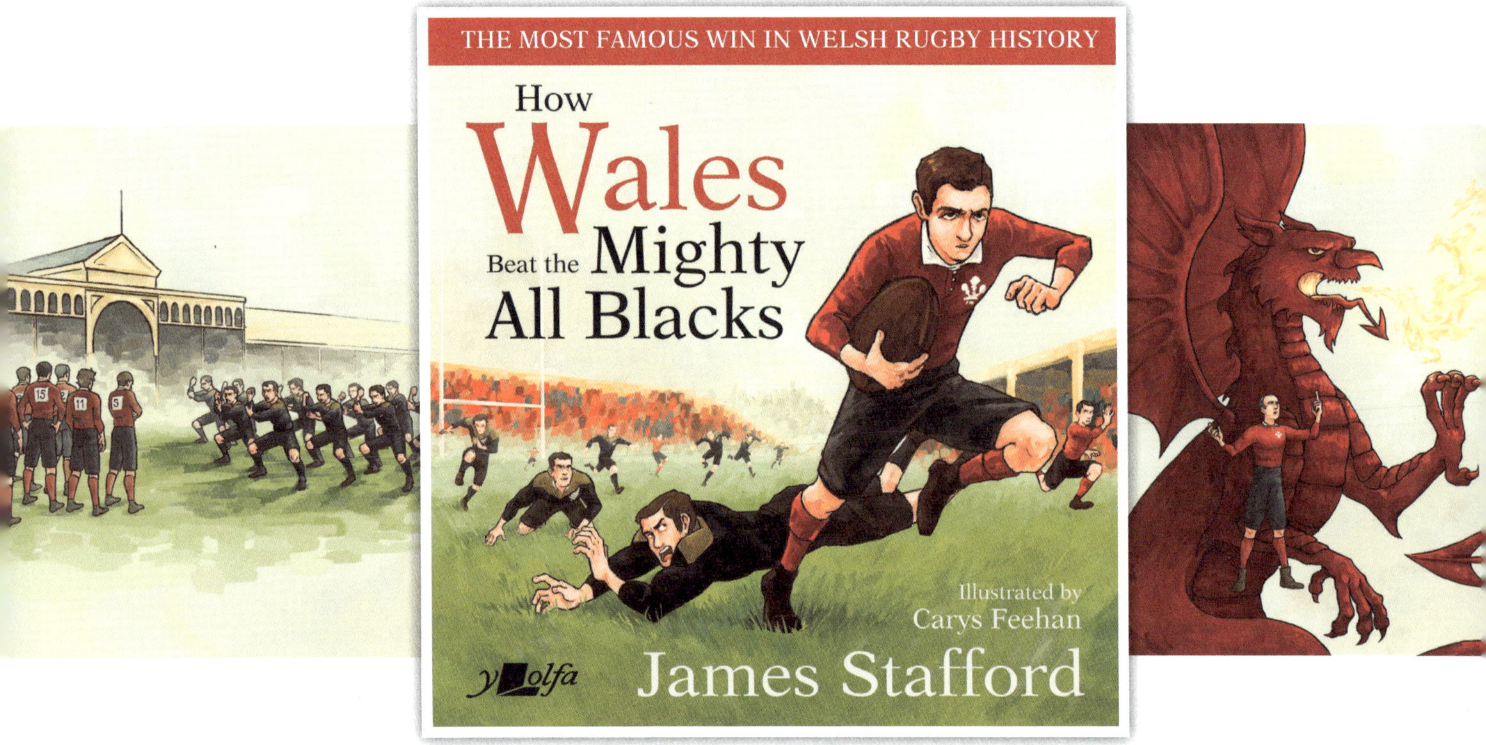

How Wales Beat the Mighty All Blacks

£7.99

How Wales Beat the Mighty All Blacks tells the fascinating true story of the first-ever clash between Wales and New Zealand in 1905. This fully illustrated hardback will appeal to children aged 7 and upwards, as well as rugby-loving adults. James Stafford's acclaimed bestseller, packed with gorgeous artwork by Carys Feehan, brings to life the most famous win in Welsh sporting history and transports readers back in time to a Wales of yesteryear.